running

is

flying

running

is

flying

Aphorisms, Meditations, and Thoughts
on a Running Life

paul e. richardson

illustrations by paul cox

RODALE.

© 2012 by Rodale Inc.
Illustrations © Paul Cox

Rodale books may be purchased for business or promotional use or for special sales. For information, please write to:

Special Markets Department, Rodale, Inc., 733 Third Avenue, New York, NY 10017

Printed in the United States of America

Rodale Inc. makes every effort to use acid-free ♾, recycled paper ♲.

Illustrations by Paul Cox

Book design by Chris Rhoads

Library of Congress Cataloging-in-Publication Data is on file with the publisher.

978–1–60961–221–4

Distributed to the trade by Macmillan

2   4   6   8   10   9   7   5   3   1   hardcover

We inspire and enable people to improve their lives and the world around them.
www.rodalebooks.com

to mom & dad

Introduction

It is 1977. We are in a dark, airless gymnasium, a creation of the previous century. Basketball practice is winding down and Coach's patience has run out.

"Enough. Baseline!"

He is a man of few words.

We hope for a bit of mercy. If he is in a good mood, Coach will only make us run quarters, where we dip and touch the lines marking each quarter length of the court before sprinting back again. Problem is, for the past century, every indoor sport known to humankind has been played in this gym, and there are about 300 horizontal lines painted across the dusty floor.

Coach is inscrutable. He takes a long time looking us up and down, considering our effort. Finally, he raises the whistle to his lips. His voice is measured, deliberate, authoritative. He pauses between each word, savoring his delivery: "Every. . . . Single. . . . Line."

And then the whistle blows.

Many of us have been saddled with the notion that running is punishment, a tool for humiliation and control. Is it any wonder that too few adults see running as something liberating and enjoyable? Or that it takes so long to get there?

In fact, many who take up running as a form of long-term fitness treat it as a self-inflicted penance—guilt mounting for every missed day, for not hitting an overly ambitious pace, for not measuring up to a PR.

This is so very, very wrong.

Running is hard work, yes. But it can also be fun and exhilarating. At its best, it recaptures the joy we experienced before running was recast as punishment, when we would sprint out of the shadows into a darkened cul-de-sac to kick a can, chase someone on the playground, or race our dog along the beach.

And while that joy can be easy to find (remember finishing your first 5-K?), it can be monumentally difficult to sustain in the face of hectic, complicated lives. Indeed, a runner's joy can be easily squelched when he realizes that finishing that first 5k is just the beginning, that running (and fitness more generally) is an endless pursuit, something you must continue to do for the . . . rest . . . of . . . your . . . life . . .

Running is not a crash diet or a quick fix. For those who take it seriously, it is a lifestyle. And for all its bone-strengthening, artery-clearing, fat-burning benefits, running is not only a *difficult* lifestyle choice, it is also a rather bizarre, eccentric one. We runners consider it normal to get up before the crack of dawn and run back and forth through the streets of our towns while the rest of the world is perfectly content to sleep another hour. We train for months to run an obscenely long distance in three or four hours, paying for the pleasure, and often we are doing it just to qualify for a chance to do it *again* under still more difficult circumstances, at an even higher price.

Yet this eccentricity is what I love about running. That plus the fact that it lets me eat pretty much whatever I want.

I also like that, as a sport, running is so natural and so simple: All we need are shoes and a pair of shorts . . . and some wicking shirts and hats, a GPS chronowatch, friction-reducing socks, an iPod, a good pair of sunglasses, a heart rate monitor, and maybe one or two other things.

It is the simplicity of this sport that gets me out of bed on those early mornings, but it is the strangeness that keeps me going on the long runs week after week. For it is this strangeness that reminds me to never, *ever* take myself or my adopted lifestyle too seriously. Actually, if I did take myself seriously, I would have to give up running, because I will never be fast or sleek or strong. Back on that high school basketball team, I was renowned for my complete lack of speed, so I know I will never win a race. But I can be persistent, and I can enjoy what I am doing.

Humor helps.

For me it does, anyway. When I run, my mind tends to wander to strange places. The aphorism, thoughts, and meditations in this book are a product of these wanderings. And of my warped world view.

It may be too much to expect that *Running is Flying* will lighten your step, lengthen your long run, or inspire a PR. But I hope it will at least provide some encouragement, and help you take yourself and this bizarre pursuit a bit less seriously. Actually, if you take nothing else away from this book, take this: Running should never be punishment. It should be enjoyable. It should make you feel like you are flying.

Because you are.

Every . . . Single . . . Mile.

Paul Richardson
Montpelier, Vermont

Almost every child can run.

Almost every adult forgets how.

Almost.

The speed of oncoming cars

is inversely proportional

to the width of the road.

Convincing sane people

to pay for the privilege of running

is the greatest scam

perpetrated on mankind

since bottled water.

Is it any wonder the two

often show up together?

Running is flying.*

*When you walk, one foot is always on the ground. When you run, most of the time you are actually airborne. For example: a 6-foot-tall runner with feet about 1 foot long was found to take 1,250 steps while running 8-minute miles. Thus, while covering 1 mile—5,280 feet—he was in touch with the ground for 1,250 feet and airborne for 4,030 feet. Put another way, he was in the air 76 percent of the time. So don't think of it as a 10-mile run. Think of it as 7 miles of flying.

Nothing makes you miss running more

than getting injured.

You don't need shoes to run

any more than you need a hat to think.

She who runs in the dark

does not have a life insurance agent

as a running partner.

If you want to be faster,

measure your runs in minutes and seconds.

If you want to be thinner,

measure your runs in cheeseburgers

and doughnuts.*

*The average man burns 124 calories each mile run; the average woman burns 105 calories. One McDonald's Big Mac = 540 calories = 4.35 miles (men), 5.14 miles (women). One Dunkin' Donuts plain glazed donut = 220 calories = 1.77 miles (men), 2.09 miles (women).

Running is like listening.

Everyone knows how to do it;

few give it the time it deserves.

Never wear a shirt

for a race you have not run.

Running is weightlifting.*

*Every stride is a takeoff. The less you weigh, the easier you will fly. In a marathon, an average runner takes about 35,000 steps, so an extra pound means lifting an extra 17½ tons over the course of 26.2 miles. For most runners, dropping 5 pounds can drop their 5-K time by a minute.

It is possible to sleep while running.

It is not possible to run while sleeping.

On an otherwise empty country road,

oncoming and passing cars

will always meet at the point

where both are passing you.

It will be on a bridge.

With puddles.

Embrace the incline.

It is not the downhills

that make you stronger.

It is better to be fast than to look fast.

You know you are running too fast

when all the butts around you

look better than your own.

Coffee is to running

as chocolate sauce is to ice cream.

You can have one without the other,

but why would you?

If running is just mechanics,

then eating is just chemistry,

and life is just days on a calendar.

The mind curses the 6 a.m. February runs.

The heart thanks you.

Never trust a runner with clean shoes.

When your second wind comes,

do not use all of it.*

*With apologies to Confucius.
("When prosperity comes, do not use all of it.")

If a runner falls in a forest

and no one is around,

she picks herself up

and never mentions it to anyone.

Yes, Virginia, people did run before BodyGlide.

They did it with blisters.

If you want to clear your head,

run alone.

If you want to be stronger,

run in a pack.

A nonrunner will never understand

the joy that running gives you.

Or the pain.

If you don't find joy in running,

don't blame the running.

Blame the you.

It's not the running you dislike,

it's the place you have put it in your life.

If you can't talk while you run,

you probably need to swallow that doughnut.

Pity the runner whose spouse

does not run.

If you are the fastest,

you don't have to be pretty or nice.

Problem is, someone is always faster.

You can never make up on the downhill

what you lose on the climb.

But you can always make up

a good story on the uphill

for why you aren't trying harder.

The only thing better than

running at sunset is

running at sunset on a beach.

With a dog.

It is the fate of heel strikers

to finance orthopedists' boats.

Ibuprofen may be more portable than ice,

but you can't make a gin and tonic

with Advil.

Whenever you can't get going,

consider the dog:

He dashes for the leash

no matter the weather.

There is a special circle in Hell

for high school coaches

who use running as punishment.

If you are too busy to run,

you are too busy.

Never go to bed with an ache unmassaged.

In a marathon, everyone hits the Wall.

You can't run around it, only through it.

DEDICATION:

Paying to run a race

even when no shirt

is involved.

The only thing worse than getting beat

by an overweight guy in a pink dress?

That guy is your dad.

The road to a PR is paved

with hellacious speed work.

Always thank race volunteers.

They could do anything they want

to the Gatorade.

Nothing finishes a run like a cold beer.

Except two.

Pamper your feet

and strengthen your core.

Or hobble across the finish

like the Hunchback of Notre Dame.

Your choice.

A runner can always spot another

in a crowd.

Runners are not superstitious.

Just careful.

It's a natural reaction

when the Forces of Darkness

are aligned against you.

A little bit of running can mask

a whole lot of shoe fetish.

Four of the sweetest words

in the English language:

Are you a runner?

The number of gadgets worn while running should never exceed the number of brains in your head.

No, you're not crazy.

It's absolutely normal to

slap bandages on your nipples,

grease up your feet and groin,

and run around in the hot sun for a few hours

with a number pinned to your chest.

Go ahead, stay in bed.

No one ever got hurt *not* running.

There are two types of runners:

those who push jogging strollers,

and everyone else.

It's pretty clear who will be in charge,

come the Apocalypse.

Some of the sweetest words come in pairs.

Second wind.

Home stretch.

Personal record.

Free beer.

You should only buy new gear

if it will make you a better person.*

*New gear *always* makes you a better person.

The treadmill is to the road

what tea is to coffee:

a lot less impact,

and far less interesting.

Of course there's a difference

between a treadmill runner

and a squirrel on a wheel.

A squirrel has four legs.

Two simple rules for running in winter:

    1. Always wear one more layer

      than you think you'll need.

    2. Don't leave the house unless

      you are smarter than the ice.*

*Ice is freakishly smart. And evil.

Fatigue is like an unwelcome in-law:

If you keep quiet, smile, and hang tough,

eventually it will leave.

The most dangerous phrase

known to runners:

How hard could it be?

You may have joined this tribe

to run off cake and ice cream.

But to rise within it,

you must run to *get* the cake

and ice cream.

Shut up and run.

Acknowledgments

A tip of the running shoe to Bob Barrett, fellow devotee of LSD (the pace, not the drug) and post-run coffee, for being a patient and constructive sounding board, editor, and cheerleader.

Eternal gratitude to my non-running wife, Stephanie—who does not complain (much) about washing sweat-soaked running gear, or about my recurring aches and pains; and to my children, Sarah and Christopher, who endure the embarrassment of their middle-aged father running around town in broad daylight.

Continued thanks to my mother, Helen, who tirelessly supported the many sports pursuits of three boys; to my father, Jim, who is still flying on the other side of 80—would that we all should be so lucky; and to my brothers Jim and Mike, who seem to have gotten first pick of the sports talent genes, but who were kind enough to leave a few for me.

Finally, a special thank you to John Atwood and Shannon Welch at Rodale, who "got" this idea and helped carry it across the finish line; and to artist Paul Cox, for his funny, richly textured illustrations.

About the Author

Paul Richardson is a writer, translator, editor and publisher. Born and raised in California, he attended college and graduate school in the Midwest (Central College and Indiana University, Bloomington). He was bitten by the Russian bug in Leningrad, in 1981, shortly after swapping his tattered down jacket for a black marketer's fur hat. In 1989 and 1990, Richardson was deputy director of one of the first successful Soviet-Western joint ventures, a publishing company based in Moscow.

He is author of *Russia Survival Guide: Business & Travel* (seven editions), as well as the recently published novel *Russian Rules*. In his day job, he is publisher of *Russian Life* magazine and a consultant to the Russian Arts Foundation and Napa Valley Festival del Sole. He writes widely on Russian culture, history and society, and is a regular commentator on Vermont Public Radio.

To cope with the unnatural concentration of things Russian in his life, Richardson runs. While he began playing sports at an early age, he did not join the running tribe until his early 40s. He has since run countless races, including at least two where there was no shirt involved. He and his wife, Stephanie, live in Montpelier, Vermont, and he writes about running and Russia at **runningisflying.com**.